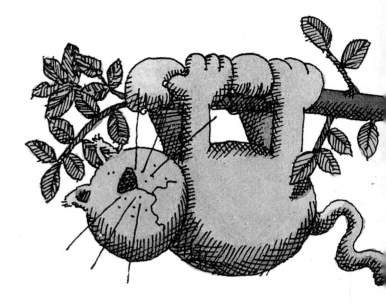

DUNDEE CITY COUNCIL

CENTRAL LIBRARY

SCHOOL LIBRARY SERVICE

Dundee
City Council
Education

To My Father
Whose Affection
for Cats is
Legendary

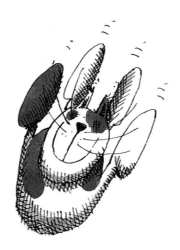

First published in Great Britain by HarperCollins Publishers Ltd in 1995. First published in Picture Lions in 1996. Text and illustrations copyright © 1995 Alan Snow
1 3 5 7 9 10 8 6 4 2 Picture Lions is an imprint of the Children's Division, part of HarperCollins Publishers Ltd. A CIP catalogue record for this title is
available from the British Library. The author asserts the moral right to be identified as the author of the work. ISBN: 0 00 664594-1 All rights reserved.
No part of this publication may be reproduced, stored in a retrieval system, or transmitted in any form or by any means, electronic, mechanical, photocopying,
recording or otherwise, without the prior permission of HarperCollins Publishers Ltd, 77-85 Fulham Palace Road, Hammersmith, London W6 8JB.
Printed and bound in Italy. This book is set in Snow Pirate Some Serif.

The·Truth·About·Cats

·by·Alan·Snow·

PictureLions

An Imprint of HarperCollins*Publishers*

Do you know where cats come from? Or what really lies beneath their soft and furry exterior? What do cats want from humans and why are dogs their enemies? To discover the fascinating story of how cats came to live on Planet Earth, what the inner workings of these curious creatures look like and why they have a secret mission, read on...

Contents

Capital city of the Planet Nip →

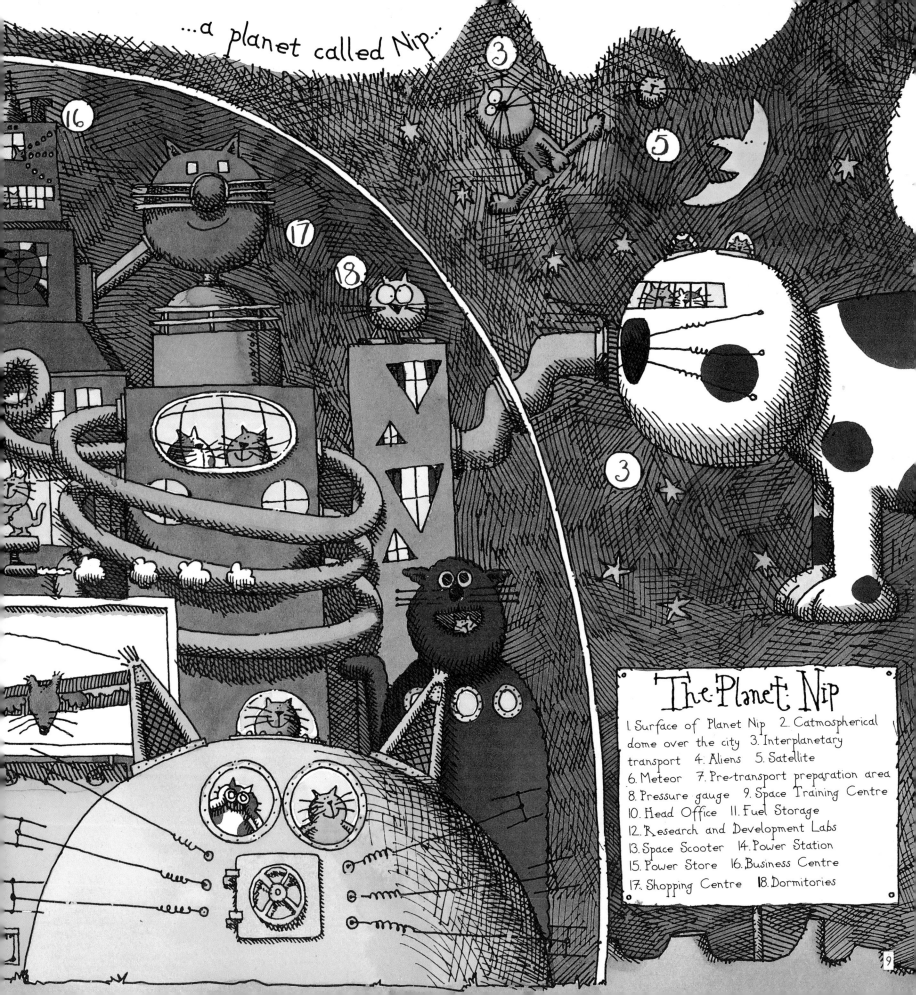

...a planet called Nip...

The Planet Nip

1. Surface of Planet Nip 2. Catmospherical dome over the city 3. Interplanetary transport 4. Aliens 5. Satellite
6. Meteor 7. Pre-transport preparation area
8. Pressure gauge 9. Space Training Centre
10. Head Office 11. Fuel Storage
12. Research and Development Labs
13. Space Scooter 14. Power Station
15. Power Store 16. Business Centre
17. Shopping Centre 18. Dormitories

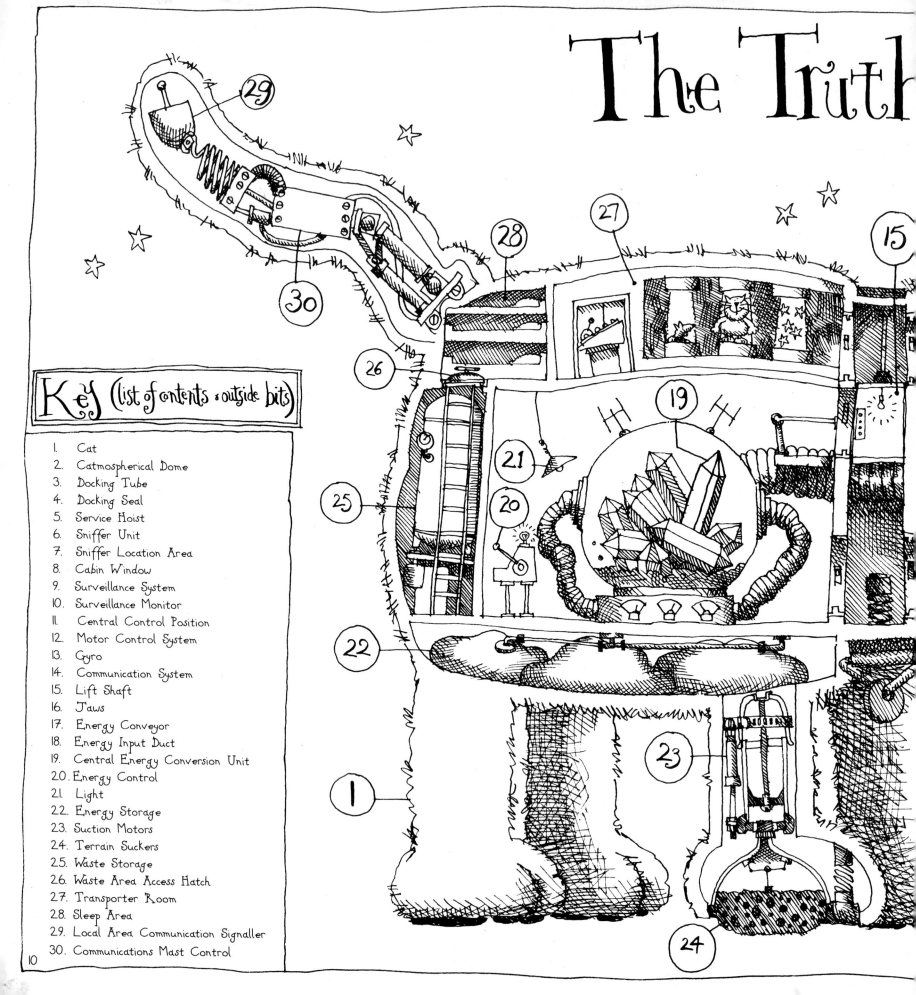

The Truth

Key (list of contents & outside bits)

1. Cat
2. Catmospherical Dome
3. Docking Tube
4. Docking Seal
5. Service Hoist
6. Sniffer Unit
7. Sniffer Location Area
8. Cabin Window
9. Surveillance System
10. Surveillance Monitor
11. Central Control Position
12. Motor Control System
13. Gyro
14. Communication System
15. Lift Shaft
16. Jaws
17. Energy Conveyor
18. Energy Input Duct
19. Central Energy Conversion Unit
20. Energy Control
21. Light
22. Energy Storage
23. Suction Motors
24. Terrain Suckers
25. Waste Storage
26. Waste Area Access Hatch
27. Transporter Room
28. Sleep Area
29. Local Area Communication Signaller
30. Communications Mast Control

About Cats

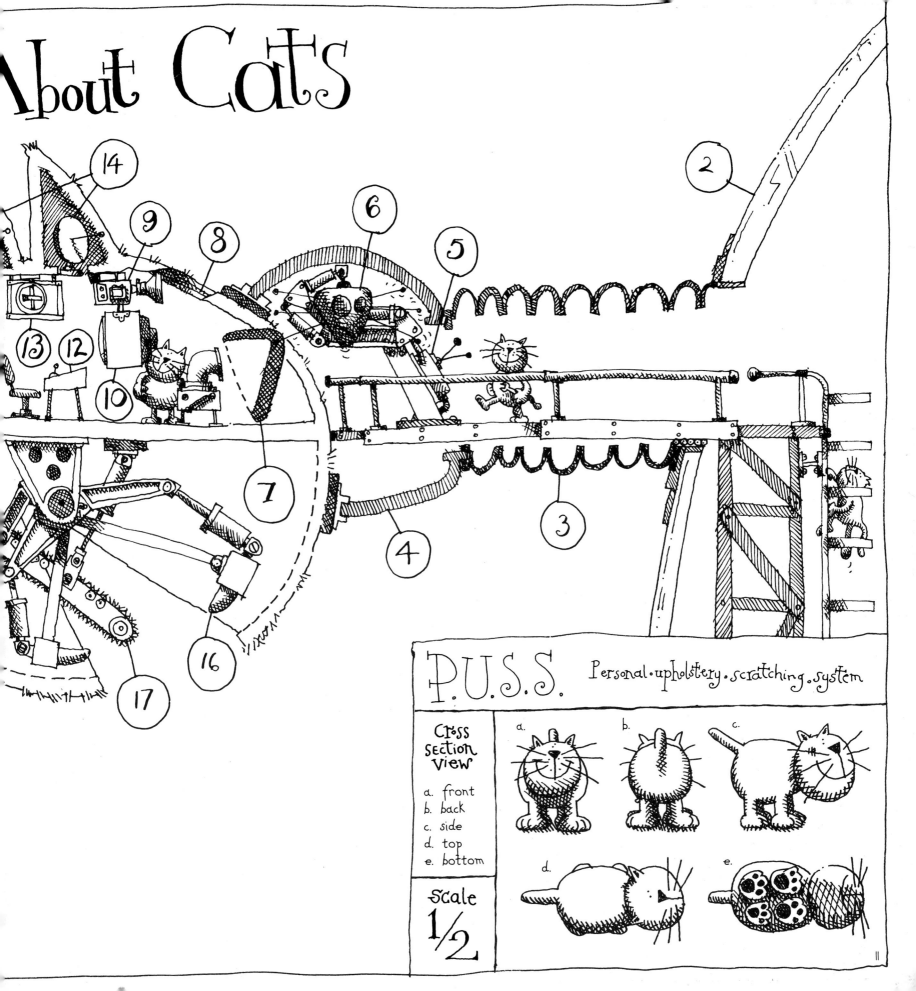

P.U.S.S. Personal·upholstery·scratching·system

Cross section view

a. front
b. back
c. side
d. top
e. bottom

Scale 1/2

Mission Earth...!?!☺☆

A long, long time ago there were two races on the Planet Nip: the Canines and the Felines. The Felines made life very miserable for the Canines by jumping on their heads and forcing them to eat fish and lick themselves clean. The Canines got so tired of this that they built a primitive space ship and set off to find a new home. After three weeks, they discovered Earth where they made friends with Humans and became known as Dogs. They settled down to a happy and comfortable life until...

communication tuner

dog scanner

lift
motor

communication headset

radar

lift

memory system

washing machine

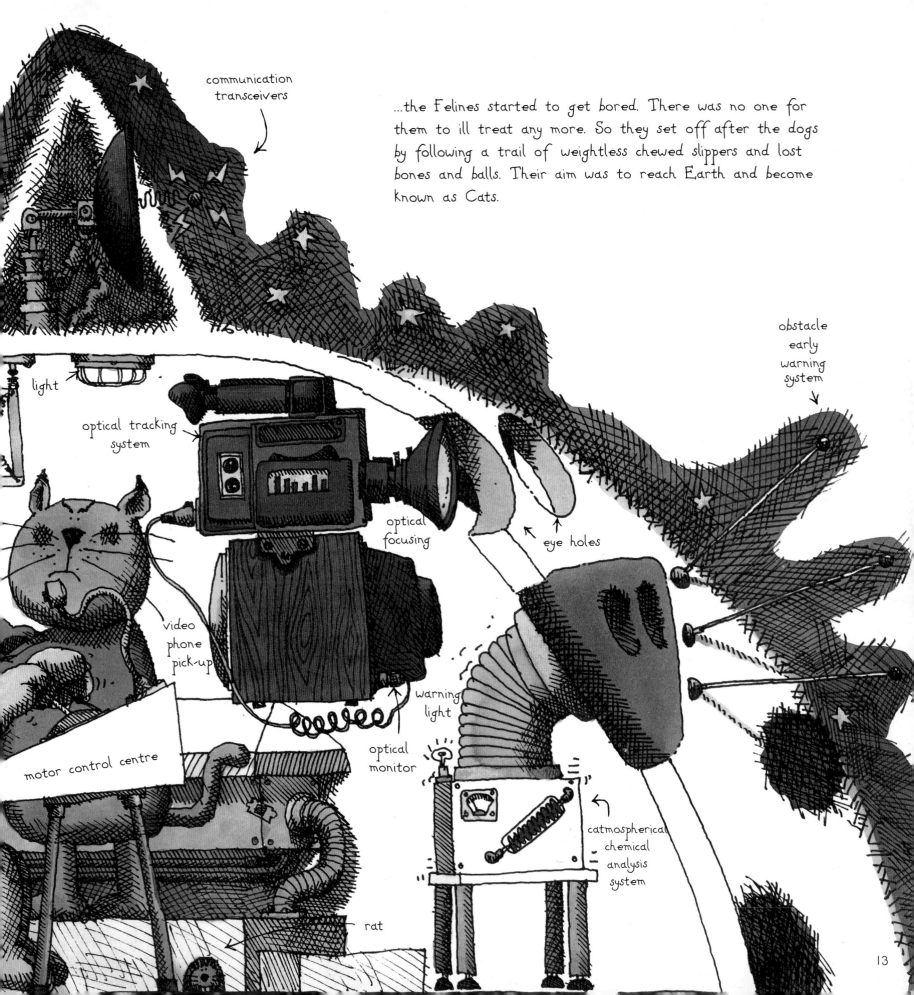

communication transceivers

...the Felines started to get bored. There was no one for them to ill treat any more. So they set off after the dogs by following a trail of weightless chewed slippers and lost bones and balls. Their aim was to reach Earth and become known as Cats.

obstacle early warning system

light

optical tracking system

optical focusing

eye holes

video phone pick-up

warning light

motor control centre

optical monitor

catmospherical chemical analysis system

rat

Space, The Final Frontier

And so the Cats made their way through the fantastic vacuum that is space, across the mighty void, weaving between stars, asteroids, planets and satellites, leaving behind the safety of home. The Cats moved ever closer to the planet Earth where the unsuspecting occupants were going about their business. Only the dogs on Earth had any idea what might happen.

Arrival on*Earth

Cats usually arrive at night so as not to arouse suspicion. A Cat who is already on the Earth's surface sends out an horrendously noisy signal to guide the orbiting Cats towards Earth. As a rule, the Cats aim to land on soft targets like compost heaps, rubbish dumps – and dogs! This can cause large quantities of dirt to become deeply embedded in the Cat's outer shell which take years for the Cat to remove. At any spare moment during a Cat's time on Earth, it can be seen trying to extract small particles of this debris from its upholstery with its 'paws' or 'mouth'.

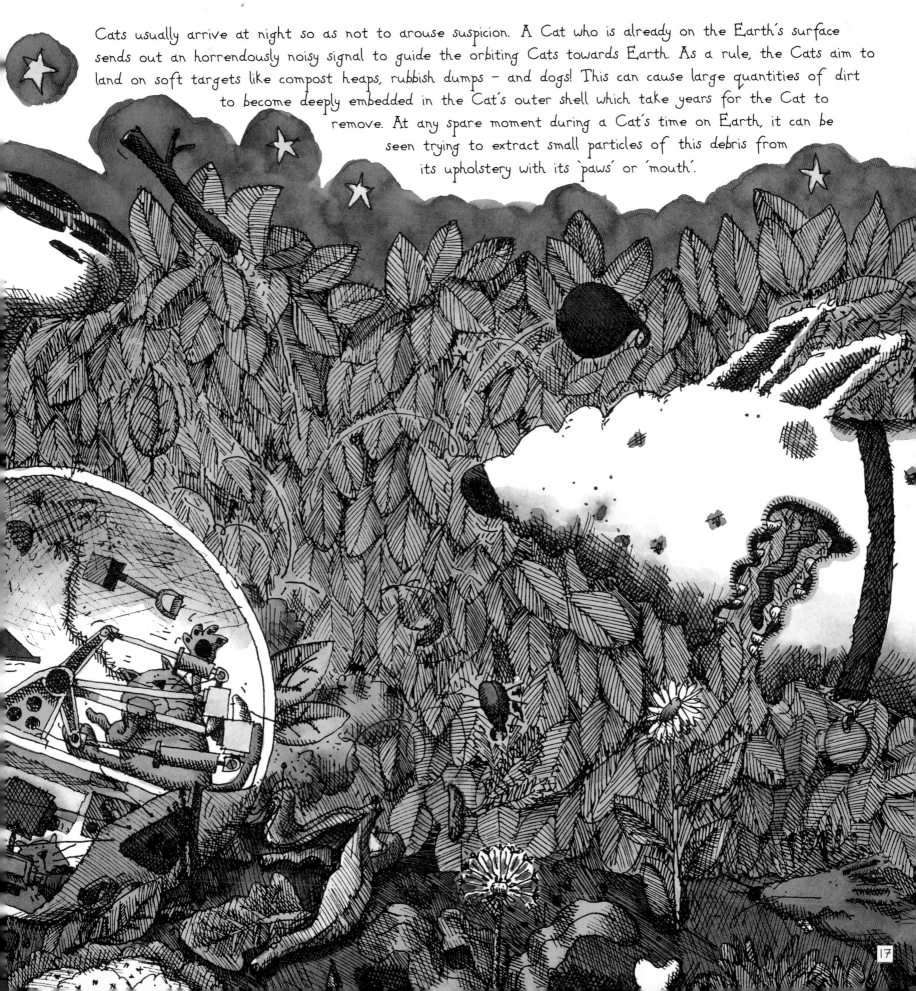

Operating on Earth

Cats and Gravity

Cats have highly strung legs that are good for hanging on to things. They also have sensors to tell which way up they are when falling. This always allows cats to fall on their feet (well, nearly always).

sensor movement

Once Cats are on Earth they use many complicated systems to get around.

positi

monitor cameras

postcard

calendar

food store

sensor alert

cooker

communicator

cat o switch

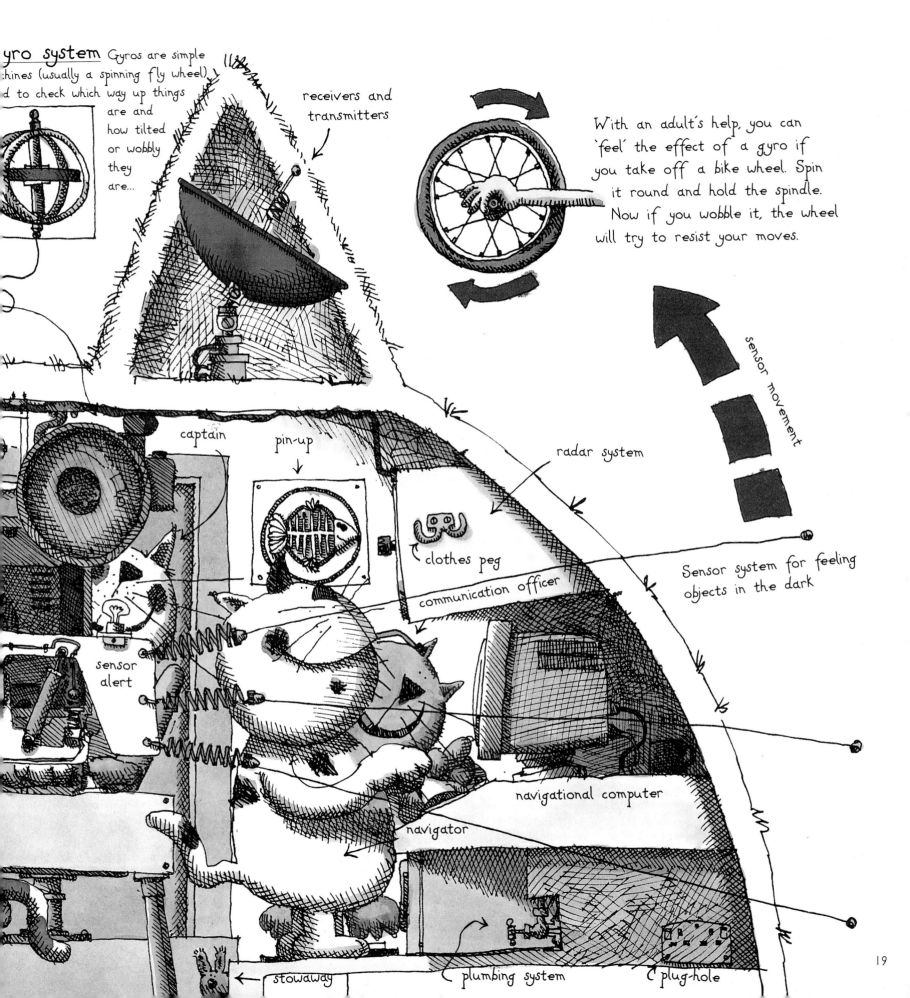

yro system Gyros are simple
achines (usually a spinning fly wheel)
d to check which way up things
are and
how tilted
or wobbly
they
are...

receivers and
transmitters

With an adult's help, you can
'feel' the effect of a gyro if
you take off a bike wheel. Spin
it round and hold the spindle.
Now if you wobble it, the wheel
will try to resist your moves.

sensor movement

captain

pin-up

radar system

clothes peg

Sensor system for feeling
objects in the dark

sensor
alert

communication officer

navigational computer

navigator

stowaway

plumbing system

plug-hole

HELP SIGNALS
(sent out to get help!)

WARNING SIGNAL!!
Surface controlled to gain volume to give illusion of greater size.

The secret and terrible mission of the Cats is wor[l]
domination and control of all fish supplies. Their fir[st]
task is to drive out all dogs. This cannot be done
just by confrontation, as dogs are usually bigger tha[n]
Cats. So Cats must use tactics...

Tactic 1

Climb into tree using suction
motors. Attract dog's attenti[on]
Wait until dog has exhausted
itself barking. Drop on dog's
head. Run away...

dog odour

Crew of Cat
ready for battle
stations.

Actions to be taken:
1. expand fur
2. up-point ears
3. retract claw covers
4. calculate size of dog an[d]
chance of good outcome in
conflict, calculate escape route
(available trees, fence, etc)
5. get legs ready
6. spit (yuk!) 7. run...

Dogs (Part 1)

WARNING SIGNAL
Ears in warning position

Tactic 2

Drive dog mad.
Move in with humans and gain their protection.
Jump on dog or steal its food while humans
are not looking. When dog reacts, wind your
Cat body around human legs.

ur inlet

Odour piped to dog brain
causes brain to go to
red alert status

dour

Tactic 3

At night, go to
house where dog lives (when
dog is locked in). Walk around yard
or garden making high pitched howling
noises that only dogs can hear. Wait until
dog has knocked him or herself insensible on
the window, trying to get you!!!

BARKING WARNING SIGNAL

Cats and Dogs (Part 2)

Inside the Cat, at the heart of the control centre...

Second in Command
Duties include standing in for Captain and general running of the Cat.

I don't like it Captain...he's too quiet...watch out for any sudden moves...

Communication Officer
Monitors audio and radio signals and reports to Captain as well as operating weapon systems – teeth, spit and claws

Open emergency channel...calling all cats

Pilot
Duties include monitoring visual path, operating legs, mouth and eating lunch.

Inside the Cat control centre the dog is monitored on the visual monitor. The monitor system can be switched to very low light levels so the Cat can operate even in darkness. The team headed by the Captain works out the best course of action...

monitor screen

dog

Don't worry... wait till he starts barking again, then full power, jump on his head and bounce over the gate!! He'll never suspect that!!

Captain
Duties include ordering equipment, reporting back to Planet Nip and choosing lunch.

Captain, I've put up the deflector shields, but I think we only have power for another three minutes.

motor control centre

Control of Humans

Humans are very easy for Cats to control. Once power is gained over them, humans are very useful for collecting food and providing protection. They can be trained to accept comings and goings at all times of day or night. This leaves Cats free to pursue their master plan of world domination and control of all fish supplies.

Some humans can even be persuaded to build escape hatches into their own buildings, especially for Cats. These should be just big enough for Cats to squeeze through but just small enough for a dog's head to get stuck. Much fun can be had with these. Cats may appear too large for the hole but this is just an illusion because they come from another planet space dimension!

Watch out for the following signs in humans - any of these show that a Cat is in control:

A weird desire to buy pretty cat collars

Speaking in 'baby talk' to adult Cats

Allowing Cats to rip up and ruin expensive furniture

Trekking around every shop in town to find just the right brand of cat food

Enthusiastic glow (radiation from sympathy ray)

A large number of Cats supported by a single human.

Some humans are very feeble minded and, in ...ese cases, total control can be gained with little ...ort. When this happens a large number of Cats ... be supported by a single person, and their every ... will be catered for...fresh fish, transport, ...niture for scratching, even total protection from ...s. Since the earliest of times, Cats have ... taking advantage of this, and throughout ...ory they have wheedled their way into positions ... power within many homes.

...n with the help of these feeble minded ...ans, Cats have not yet succeeded in ... mission. But, day by day, they gain ... power. Their numbers are ...tiplying and their hold over ...ans and dogs is strengthening. ...s are already banned from ... public places, while Cats roam ...ely wherever they want. So be ...ned – complete Cat control ...ot far away!

The End

Index

Look out for HOW DOGS REALLY WORK, the hilarious companion volume to THE TRUTH ABOUT CATS, essential for all wary pet owners.

HOW Dogs Really Work!

BY·Alan·Snow

Available from Collins Children's Books in hardback, paperback and miniature hardback